Animal Like Any Other

poems by

Tara Shea Burke

Finishing Line Press
Georgetown, Kentucky

Animal Like Any Other

ACKNOWLEDGMENTS

many of these poems were published as earlier versions in form and content
and many thanks to the following journals and publications for giving them
homes

Sinister Wisdom, Reading Queer: Poetry in a Time of Chaos edited by
Maureen Seaton and Neil de la Flor, published by *Anhinga Press;* Split This
Rock Poetry Contest judged by Mark Doty; *Adrienne: A Poetry Journal of
Queer Women* from Sibling Rivalry Press; *Tinderbox Poetry Journal; Minola
Review; The Fem, Lavender Review; Public Pool; Whale Road Review; Yes,
Poetry; Glass Poetry Journal; South Florida Poetry Journal; Rogue Agent;
Punch Drunk Press*

"The Blueberry Syrup" was inspired by Tim Seibles' poem "The Applecake."

Publisher: Leah Maines
Editor: Christen Kincaid
Cover Art: A.E. Hinson
Author Photo: Marissa Johnson
Cover Design: Elizabeth Maines McCleavy

Printed in the USA on acid-free paper.
Order online: www.finishinglinepress.com
            also available on amazon.com

Author inquiries and mail orders:
Finishing Line Press
P. O. Box 1626
Georgetown, Kentucky 40324
U. S. A.

Table of Contents

Comfort Food 1

Good and Holy 3

Blue Ridge Mountain Road 5

Fall 8

Earliest Memory 10

Home 11

How We Purpled the Road 13

What Was In Front of Us 16

Even Though I Knew Nothing was Certain 18

Letter to My Father/Elegy to the Not Yet Dead 20

Inside Me 22

When the Heart is Heavy 24

New Year's Day 26

Dreamwork or Love 28

Seven Years 29

For More 30

After the Move 31

Who Lives and Who Dies 33

Praise Song 34

In Defense 35

After the Breakup 36

Away 37

Burn It Down 38

Declaration 40

Stories I Told 42

Exercise in Which a Poet in Heartbreak Finds Herself in a
  Writing Class with Fiction Writers and Doesn't Leave,
  Rebels a Little, Learns to Put Characters Under Pressure 44

Transformation 49

Queer Girl 50

Blueberry Syrup 52

Let Us Live 56

Blue Body Hungry for Origin or Certainty 57

Dear Me As I Try To Remember Something About Love 62

Goat Memory 66

*for my family and all the strange days we made
into something like love on Blue Ridge Mountain Road*

The body knew the body
would dream of headlessness the way
a breast dreams of bra-lessness of blouselessness
of sunlight and weightlessness
The body knew that someday
it would have to move to forget to
dance to forget that it knew
what it knew

-Tim Seibles

Comfort Food

In the gray house we ate big dinners on gray or blue plates. On the gray or blue plates in the gray house with the brown carpet and tan couches we sat and ate big dinners. Meat and potatoes, mashed and covered in cheese and butter and cream and we ate it all on the tan couch in the gray house with the brown carpet and the television at eye level, our bodies curled in, plates balanced on our laps. Sometimes we talked on the tan couch with the blue or gray plates on our curled in legs balancing red meat cooked gray and tan mashed potatoes and boiled green beans that were barely green. Sometimes we talked or laughed or dad would make a bird call or fart noise and The Simpsons were on commercial break and all our curled-in bodies would laugh as we shoveled meat and potatoes and green beans into our mouths.

Sometimes Shane would sit with me in front of the television before dinner and ignore mom's yell to not ruin our dinner and we'd roll Fruit by the Foot into big gooey baseballs of fake fruit snacks in our hands and we'd ignore mom and the television was in our faces and Shane would burp the ABCs as we swallowed Coke and Fruit by the Foot and waited for the big plates of meat and beans and potatoes and more Coke or milk and big sighs from our parents in their respective spots on the couches. The television told us what happened in DC that day even though we were an hour a way in the gray house on Blue Ridge Mountain Road and we watched the news together and all agreed politicians were liars and dad said *what a bunch of baloney* and we laughed and agreed and shoved food into our mouths from the couch or the brown carpet laughing and rolling around, sticking our toes onto the television, shoving big toes into politicians noses as mom made something in the kitchen probably meat and potatoes and boiled canned green things.

One day and all days she was too tired and dad never made food except that one time he tried to teach me how to make scrambled eggs we added milk did we add milk who adds milk to scrambled eggs? But this one day of many tired days dad was probably at his night job and mom worked at Mott's Applesauce factory in Winchester, Virginia, and watched as some people's fingers slipped under the belts and some ladies came in smoking their next cigarette while the one they just smoked burned between their fingers and *how could they have hickeys on their necks* she laughed, that same story I heard so many times about old wrinkled women in Disney sweatshirts with hands pressing plastic into machines and cigarettes hanging out of their mouths and *hickeys on their necks somehow,* she'd say, perhaps to keep herself separate, or perhaps because she never understood that sex still happened for most people.

She must have been tired, so many times. And I wasn't allowed to stay home alone with Shane anymore we were too young and I got into the knives so she must have been tired and only dad worked the night shift now so mom, *MOM can we make our own dinner tonight? Oh god yes please make your own dinner tonight* but the problem was no one was awake enough to show us how. No one was awake enough to show us how in the house on Blue Ridge Mountain Road with so many odd jobs at odd hours and odd factories and night shifts and meat and potatoes and boiled cans of green things and me and those knives so what's one night she must have asked as we poured a half gallon of the cheapest skim milk from Food Lion into a big glass bowl on the brown carpeted floor in front of the television, The Simpsons on—our cultural commentary, or Fox news to scoff at before it was Fox news to scoff at and our little bodies and hairy legs formed a half-moon too close to the screen but clearly we did what we wanted on those nights, the nights where someone was home but too tired and I couldn't boil water or be trusted with knives so Nabisco Honey Maid graham crackers and Food Lion brand skim milk in a big bowl as mom ate her own meal and laughed, warned us we'd be sick on Blue Ridge Mountain Road in the gray house on the brown carpet, milk splashing, our little fingers floating boats of Nabisco Honey maid graham crackers on the sea of milk, the blue light of the television an illumination, our open mouths two baby birds eager until we were so full and sickly sweet we couldn't stand another bite, but there were no boundaries here so our bodies and bellies pressed forward and we laughed and laughed until it was gone, round-bellied rebels in the gray house surrounded by trees miles away from anyone else on Blue Ridge Mountain Road

Good and Holy

When I am dead please mourn
by spending too many days in bed
with the dogs and your laptop.
Stream whatever you damn well please,
even those awful cop shows you love.
Get angry at weird things, like my stack
of dusty books I never read, your body
as it awakens to future lovers,
our rarely-used dildos and toys.
When you are the most rage-sad,
reach for the tiny vibrator
in your underwear drawer,
the one you caught me using
even though I have my own
and make yourself come
until it hurts. This will be good
and holy. Normal. I'd want your grief
so queer. When I am dead please
don't let anyone put my dead body
in a casket or church and don't let
my yoga friends chant anything I
wouldn't chant: empty phrases like
*she's gone back to the light from which
she came,* even though I've said
that dumb shit before. I want so badly
to be burned Viking-style out at sea,
or on some mountain river raft
and yes, my desire to be a dead body
on fire made us laugh, but please
know I meant it. I want this body
finally mine, naked, covered
in glitter and chicken feathers,
placed on fresh, imperfectly cut
logs, tied together with scraps
of yarn and twine, and burst
into flames. Douse me
in expensive red wine. If you

can stomach it, light the end
of a whiskey-soaked arrow
and shoot. I know how alive
you feel with a weapon
in hand, how you'll never
resist a worthy shot.

Blue Ridge Mountain Road

Maybe it's what we don't say
that saves us.
-Dorianne Laux

the clustered row of mailboxes up the thick-graveled driveway the clustered row a patch of metal and plastic on wooden stakes I'd skip to some Saturday mornings when mom would shoo me away *go get the mail* and I'd open and close and open and close all the boxes after mom told me not to after mom told me it was illegal I opened them all because everything felt closed all evidence of other people living nearby other families like us hidden in houses down thick-graveled driveways or up depending on which side of the road you were on all of these boxes a row of them proof of other life nearby the big metal green one the size of a small dog my favorite the green of it beside all the black and gray and white Washington Post newspaper plastic sleeve boxes the enormous green one I imagined I could fit inside almost 16 years there and I never saw anyone open it everything so closed and covered by the woods and privacy but there was life nearby even though it felt like just the four of us the road to Mt. Weather the top of our mountain on Blue Ridge Mountain Road

at the bottom of our thick-graveled driveway was our gray house the little rambler and the green yard and the thicketed clearing where dad placed a homemade birdhouse and seed and our well pump and the garden or the rock garden or the rocks and the garden around it or what lasted of the garden and what mom planted what mom planted was wildflowers and lilies and azalea bushes and over the years she stopped cultivating or weeding but we didn't believe in weeds we lived in the woods we knew what was supposed to grow and grow over and die on its own and when to leave the leaves and when to blow them all away but the pink and yellow miracle of the lilies and azaleas every year the mess of it and color and her stones collected from the woods when she could still move around lift things bend over and place them here and there intending toward beauty the hills unleveled we lived in the woods we only wanted to level so much a landscape like a forest we lived with but when I drove home those last times before she left it to the mold to the bank those stones still nestled on the hill across the yard and gravel driveway the stones nestled like a thousand dead camels buried to their humps in the earth

I can still see the light from my father's bedside lamp at dusk the house on Blue

Ridge Mountain Road a ghost in my mind a thing we all ran from left mom to care for as the pipes leaked and the basement flooded and the walls crawled with black mold and no one could stand it could go home and save it we all tried to save it didn't we didn't my father as he lay in bed every night no not quite night it was dusk then we were small and his work was early so his bed was early and we never once put a curtain on the windows mom thought blinds were ugly as hell or tacky the trees covered us mostly but in winter the light burned from the road up the gray gravel driveway and once I was not small and could drive I felt so big and alive but I was still small I drove and drove and came home late at night always pushing hours past my curfew but no one called it curfew so hours past after school in winter close to dusk probably darker in winter I could see him tucked in shirtless and hairy as a beast what a mountain man the glow of his bedside lamp and the empty bed beside him I see him there alone in that king-sized bed with space left for mom up until he said fuck it and started drinking again pushed past dusk and then duskier and after he said fuck it this was after we left he plucked the guitar again because what was left after the kids were gone was a big bed and mom on the couch still but back then when I could see him from the road he read into the dark he read by the light his early rise a twenty-year love song to our family he rose sometimes at 3 no 4 am and he left the guitar in its case under the bed and his passion for life was a scream in his gut an ulcer a song he couldn't sing oh I see him there a book in his hand sober and tired and quiet like most alcoholics when they keep the nectar out of their mouths to try so hard to keep relationships alive

I can still hear us all trying to find a way to joy my mother so quick at the subject change so quick to find a way to make us laugh it could be the right sitcom turned up loud at the right time or a warm moment with my father some bird noise or snide at the dumb shit on television or my father's farts or stinky feet the room filled with smells of a man in boots all day a family stuffing it all down every meal every television show every homework assignment every idea mom on the couch her big 7-11 mug filled with ice and generic diet coke and all our dramas for no reason I hated her spot on the couch and her loud insistence on my homework her insistence on our thinking brains and entertained brains being one in the same for so long I hated her change of the subject her love of story because I can't remember a time the television wasn't on in front of her in front of us but I go back now I go way back and I remember her on my little oak trundle bed and the pink quilt and my stacks and stacks of books for Book-

It and mom there with me which book should we read today which 3 books 4 books 5 books 6 books don't forget to mark it down let's read Tara let's read aloud let's laugh and make voices and use our imagination and here is a pen and paper and let's drive to school down this long mountain road and practice our times tables I have a song we can sing a mnemonic device yes mne-mon-ic device we can use to remember what are the state capitals do you remember our song Tara what can we repeat and rhyme and sing to or make up in our heads the world is an endless rhymed song you make up in your head until you have made the world and for many years I looked back at all the television drugs in my system and scoffed and judged and shamed her on that couch but oh she sang a love of narrative of story of sound and all things pop and culture into my bones she sang it all we read it loud we read and we read and I thought we had so little but maybe we had it all

dear reader what I can say is how all I wanted was to remember the trees and the fall the orange and the leaves the memory of fall in my mind how the leaves fall they fall they still fall they are always falling once I wanted to sing this as ode to trees to the orange in my mind to the fire the light the laughter everything you can see and can't say from the outside the gray house the thick gravel the light most lit from afar from above the house on Blue Ridge Mountain Road

Fall

When we met we fell for each other like leaves.
Behind black curtains her bedroom was dark
except for the soft surprise of pale yellow walls.
Her dogs laid behind the closed door,
waiting to be let back in between us.
Paws and little whines inched under the door
toward the warm light of our wanting.
After, we became four bodies intertwined:
legs, breasts, fur, sheets—all sleepy and sweet
snoozing until the bedroom's next dark noon.
We slipped pink steaks between wine-stained
teeth one autumn night in the new of us.
We chewed and chatted, a bit tipsy
by her fire pit. I remember the slow
getting-to-know-yous there, whatever
necessary to make nights more than sex.
And then, between bloody bites, I asked
why on earth would you want to fight in Iraq?
knew the wrong answer might set me off,
make me primal—an animal wanting
no more than a few tipsy urge-easing
evenings—if I'm honest I wanted
a reason to go. Her answers surprised me,
taught me more than I'd bargained for,
the old me ready to run with one wrong answer
about war. My desire for a long love, something
I'd never had, made my body an ear, a sheath
of skin on guard—a forest at midnight—somewhere
I'd never been before. And then her body, her military
stance, her want apparent but hidden just enough: a ship
at sea, on radar but silent, floating   oh all of this
suspended me, suspense enough to fall hard.
I worried that I'd turn cold—a dry
winter earth, cracked and frozen from holding in all
my protest. Instead, I followed fire to the bedroom,
and again. I expected the slow honey we made
to cool off, change shape. But I ate

the thick sugar and let go. I dreamt of her
behind safe steel walls at sea—
not active but present—her work
in taking down American-made enemies.
Woke in the dark, touched her skin.
For a moment, I understood her service
like most things alive in the raw honey
between extremes. Oh time, oh back story,
oh what I fell for surrendered to shut
my mouth for oh how we fell—
two women finding something like love
or comfort in differences. In overlaps.
The sweet burn of sun on our skin
as we fell to the ground.

Earliest Memory

bright kitchen table in Nags Head North Carolina on one of very few family vacations before baby brother his name not yet a conversation before half brothers stopped coming to stay we sat at the table the bright kitchen table with the white tile floor beneath our baby feet our child feet our dangling feet my chubby thighs piano thighs houses for my toddler feet sticking out and dangling down and around like it's the best thing Hi-C juice box in my chubby toddler hand the boys at the table mom wandering around cutting crusts off white bread sandwiches Dad on the porch he is smoking the ocean is waiting for our bodies for lunch to be over we are all waiting to do something to become something a wait that will never end Dad sighs looks out and around the sea the sky the family he made then the second family he made here too beside the half brothers who stopped coming to stay and Mom's in that blue leopard print ruffled one-piece to hide what she thought was post-me fat a linger around the middle most women were and still are afraid of but the fear was small here her long hair in the side French-braid she always wore and our happiness here too still vulnerable to the light pouring in the light a thing I still seek the illumination of banal but the soft middle of her body the thing the metaphor for all that was to come but no not here this meal this table this tiny ordinary moment in time true the sunlight true Mom's happiness true too our young family without boundary or fortune or any idea what struggle what unmet longing what desires would die ignored and I am just a chubby child unaware of chubby unaware of what piano legs mean or thunder thighs just happy and kid-fat with my juice here a squeal in my mouth and then a squeeze in my hand as pink splashes my white high chair and the white tiled floor and perhaps no I know this is the beginning my first yes to the *just do it* in my rebellious bones my *push it see what happens* and oh how I still love this urge the test the gush the spilling over out of straws jeans bodies mouths the messes we make so I squeeze again and again until I hear STOP and I don't then TARA I SAID STOP and I shake unclear of no and its partner shame stunned as this better world is shut for me this dimension I still flirt toward where we squeeze what we want to squeeze just to see what happens celebrate and mom squeezes back and we all laugh joy unfettered and roll around in the sugary stick of what is spilled and reflected there

Home

The lesbian leans against the kitchen sink washing dishes.
The other lesbian climbs a ladder outside against the back of the house.
The door is open, and today is Spring.
The end of the first warm day after weeks of snow and melt.
Their dogs play rough in the mud.
Baby birds crack their little blue shells from the inside.
Neighbors are in the street.
They toss beanbags into Cornhole boards and drink beer.
The sun sets later than the day before.
It drops behind rows of houses.
The dogs come in and out through the mudroom, across the linoleum and tan carpets.
The dogs have muddy paws.
Crisp air follows.
The lesbian washing dishes covers her body in a sweater and readies dinner.
The other lesbian tinkers with new LED patio sensor light and rolls up her flannel shirt sleeves.
The dogs come close to the ladder and she asks her lover to keep them from knocking her off.
The lesbian agrees, but knows their dogs will run wild until tired.
She gave up any notion of clean floors years ago.
She can almost taste the atmosphere as it shifts into season—an early spring-green.
Just-lit barbeque stoves from the surrounding city.
Brussels sprouts, onions and garlic tossed in heaps of seasoning and olive oil, roasting.
Dried chicken in a dish with salt and pepper, cayenne and garlic, a little whole-wheat flour. Butter in a hot iron pan melts for the sear.
Earlier, the lesbians took apart their tub faucets.
The one fixing the light fixed their pipes and shower.
A week ago, she replaced their kitchen sink.
Last summer she taught herself how to patch cracks with drywall and install a bathroom vanity. She often fixes her lover's car and takes apart the brakes, exhaust, tie rods, all of it.
Early in their relationship, they put up a chain link fence on a hot spring day.
The dishes lesbian had a hangover—she didn't really want to carry eighty-pound bags of cement.

She wasn't ready to dig such deep holes by hand.
Wanting to be loved will make you sweat and fill the blue wheelbarrow anyway.
They played loud music and finished the job, tanning in the sun on a day like
    today.
Some days, they tangle their legs on the couch, shut the curtains, order pizza.
They snuggle dogs until their backs are stiff and there's nothing left to watch.
Others, they repaint the porch, drive for a long hike, make dinner from scratch.
They go to bed just after dusk in a quiet room with worn bodies and books.
They roll over wordless, skin-to-skin.
The cooking and washing dishes lesbian watches the tinkerer and fixer-upper.
She passes wrenches and brad nail guns.
She was good at keeping company.
She was good at tidying up around the projects.
She was good at learning a little.
But mostly she was good at simply keeping space.
She collected images, only these left.
What is left.
They built their chicken coop.
Let their home fill with tiny chirps and farm smells for weeks.
Five fluffy chicks stayed warm, grew safely indoors.
The lesbians ate their eggs, shared costs of animal care.
They didn't want children, or marriage.
They wanted choice.
They wanted home.
Space, and this simple bliss.
Those chosen days, gone now, and each other.
Each other.

How We Purpled the Road

has the world gone mad, or is it me?
all these small things, they gather round, they gather round me
          -Ben Howard

you are the one I want to come home to now baby brother your little purple face on my four-year-old lap wailing wailing I always remember you wailing and most the time it was me but it couldn't have been then you were a newborn on my lap home from the hospital bottle in my hand in your mouth your open mouth wailing I remember sitting there or is it the photo that thrusts this memory how much of this is real I was smiling with your bottle in my hand and you wailed and then later your black belly-button in my palm as it shriveled there in my open palm then on an oak bookshelf by your crib no matter how hard I try I can't remember ever looking through your crib bars any other day except the day dad came home very late and very drunk how did he make it up the dark mountain road it doesn't matter I was four and you were new and after that night after the fist in the drywall and the lights on and mom's face not hit but the threat of the hit lingering and dad asleep in the basement the next morning everything became sober for a very long time but I remember you wailed that night too and mom either brought me to your crib bars or I stood there or I'm imagining it and we were just you and me and mom in my room on the pink quilt or in her room on the blue quilt somewhere we sat together and cried and felt fear that no one named but I know now this fear was how do we embody this family how does this house hold us did it ever hold all our real or silent wailing

and then you are older but still a baby still a child still new in mom's arms on the tan couch with Dr. Kerns' orders to push gently push gently with force a gentle force push with force but gently a blunt needle a very blunt object like a needle into your tiny baby penis because peeing was painful because peeing was a struggle because you wailed and wailed and your urethra was too small too small for anything to come through with ease oh brother I have written this poem one hundred times and only now do I understand that it was your body not mine I always thought it was mine but your body your tiny wailing body was the one our family pushed gently with force over and over what was supposed to come forth our wasted water wasted milk wasted ingestion but no I watched as she pushed it through like only a mother could she both held and soothed your pain while making it and later up and down our driveway our gravel driveway that curved in and out of our home like a ventricle like vena cava like what must be pumped in must also pump out like what keeps us alive could also smother us drown us in blood or oxygen or too much too much I don't know how to tell true stories about you but I do see us kicking gravel and playing *Tremors* on the big rocks in dad's blazed trails his footpaths in the woods made for us this is what he made for us and on big boulders and trails whacked by dad his weed whacker a tool I can't ever get out of my head help me Shane how many Saturdays or Sundays did dad spend blazing the woods around our house holding the tool made to clear made to make space made to blaze I've held one many times in my own hands in awe because my forearm no matter how strong cramps but dad had his goggles on and his skinny legs in size 28 Levi's and his tan boots like the kind you wear now and I'm sure he wore other tees but the white Eagles concert tee sticks to me how the eagle faded how it always sounds like they're dead when you and I talk about them or when I try to remember the world we grew up in the yard and the woods and dad whacking weeds and you and I on the driveway up and down on our bikes and trikes and mom inside in front of the tv but the windows wide without curtain or blind watching us watching us

and I do remember your training wheels is this how I remember how often we'd walk our bikes and trikes to the top of the driveway on Blue Ridge Mountain Road and then fly down fast so fast the only way to ride them on our only road no sidewalks the paved road above too dangerous and our bikes weren't made for trails so to the top and down again we'd go over and over until one day we raced past the trees and ditches and summer Blackberries purpling the road they purpled everything the thickets and brambles and gray gravel we raced on our hands earlier but this day some angry primal mountain beast something loud and violent and surprising and familiar came undomesticated out of me she exploded from my body in a rage in a need to wreck you and let's not pretend I didn't wreck you more and maybe this is why I struggle with truth that day I rammed my front tire into your training wheels or between them and yes I knew what would happen even as I regretted it *I did* the moment your body went flying from your trike seat my beast was quiet something human in me knew evil a taste a ripe fruit a purple bruise I still remember the grind of my teeth the grip of my hand on my pink handle bars rubber grips because I grip like this still when I want to destroy something destroy myself and there you were on the gravel wailing your chin bloodied and your body already a bruise a bruise you must carry not just the one I gave you but all the purple in us all the desire and the fruits in our hands and tongue and your baby body in mine

immediate regret is a bruise I know well as well as the face of those I've let see my beast is it *our* beast don't you have stories too of the rage our basement bred or did I breed this in us in our basement left alone with kitchen knives and nights when mom and dad had to work and I'll never forget the disgust on your face the face you still carry the face that sees me with awe and something like *she is dangerous and follows through*

can I share more all our days unsupervised in the woods the branches slapped back in your face the many demands to bring me sodas and snacks and hide until I never ever come find you the panic I'd wait for then comfort what more can I say except somehow you'd wake up and say *let's go play Tara let's go play* and there was no beast just our bodies on bikes and trikes and the softening purples and mom's reminder that you'd grow up and get me back one day after all the *Tara what did you do to him nows* and you and me up the driveway and down with cups in our hands collecting ripe blackberries popping the bubbly skin into our mouths reciting lines from movies making up stories avoiding the lava streams between boulders leaving what we couldn't eat to ripen in the sun as we ran back to the front door for dinner peaceful and strange alone on our mountain everything else left in the sun we left it all in the ditch by the driveway and the deer and foxes and black bears came at night and ate what we left behind

What Was In Front of Us

Out in a field our dogs run and run,
houses in the near-distance, tree-line covering
the backyards of other dogs. The Siberian husky
is on a long-line. The old dog can roam some,
but give him a little freedom and he's gone.
Your favorite: the smart, Australian cattle herder,
is off-leash but only listens to you, comes
when you call, sits when you say sit. She is
your true match. I watch the two of you
as the sun sets at the end of a year. She heels
and you reward her from the multi-pocketed
tactical training vest I bought you for Christmas.
The one you asked for. The way love
becomes *what do you want this year?*
The fading light is behind two trees,
dancing black silhouettes, They are bare
and it is cold and they aren't the only ones
reaching. Our other dogs are in the car.
They bark and whine from the kennels
you built from scratch in the garage
as I watched you work, your perfect
dyke breasts tight behind a sports bra
and an old pair of Navy coveralls.
I am struck by the scene of us
in this field. The uncertainty of this sunset
and our next steps. Who will we be
in 365 days? We'll move to New Mexico.
Your family will be close, down the long dirt roads
between us. You'll wear a new uniform, a new
badge on your breast, a rookie deputy in the year
after Ferguson and a chokehold held
and held. How will you see this world
with your gun? Is there anything
we can protect? They say nothing good
comes of worry and I know I'm holding on
too tight. It's hard to even say I want this
but I am going with you. The sun

disappears in front of us and before it's too dark,
we pack up all our love into cars and drive home.

Even Though I Knew Nothing was Certain

I dreamed I was searching for certainty

my lover left me alone in an enormous parking garage   men were fixing cars

I climbed endless levels of cement to find her   I was naked

then in a hotel hallway that was also endless with nothing

to cover me but a tiny wet white washcloth   I turned corners

wandered corridors   wound up stuck in elevators where no one

was worried   I believed that she was one step ahead ready to pick me up

which was true   then we were in a mall holding hands

old women suddenly unsure of all the styles   people   noise

a young lesbian couple followed us   teased our clothes but this was about

temptation   one of us was lured away   and as if on replay the one who chose
to stay

became the one who strayed   what I mean is I can't stop dreaming about that
old

tired apple   the red red shine of infidelity of hunger of a body this body

she always wants more   worries her lover does too

because I do   then I was saying *yes* to a no-face no-gender body that wanted
me

we came together like it was my only chance to stray   I felt my lover

bodiless like atmosphere   the morning came   I woke with guilt and a leftover

throb of being wanted   I was sad so I reached for her unsure if I was reaching
for her

to stay or to say go   a constant worry that she turned a corner   never said

goodbye   it's true suffering   is impermanence   I want to stay put when
everything

is change or I want to be taken because I can't quite say

I want   please   let me go

I keep dreaming   endless winding corridors

parking garages   always lost   forever sad in crowds of people

who are not lost   everything seems fine so I hide in elevators

hope to god the ride takes me somewhere   without want

Letter to My Father/Elegy to the Not Yet Dead

I am standing beside you
in front of our gray house.
I am five. My acid-washed,
Sherpa-lined demin jacket, little
jeans, and you in all your denim, too.
Cigarette between your teeth,
large green cylindrical coffee thermos
in your hand. It is open, the heat
is captured in time. This
is the photograph I look to
when therapy comes to a halt.
You stare at the very working class
snowman we have built together.
I hand you the carrot.
My face says *pay attention.*
You do, just not
to me. To the sky,
as I do now.
Any horizon
in front of you.
I am still that girl.
I struggle to feel
whole. I beg everyone
who says they love me
to look. We are frozen in time.
The snowman has stuck grass
poking out of its happy cheeks.
It must have been warm,
not much snow left around us.
Just you and I and the sun setting
orange behind our little home,
the smoke from the woodstove
pressing into a gray sky by our gray house.
Wet grass and snow, mud and rocks.
I don't know how to write to you.
I see your curls every time
I look into the mirror. Feel your love

of a long buzz every time I stay up
drinking whiskey, music on, writing.
I am searching for the father
inside. What is there to say
except I might be another lesbian
with daddy issues. Though
to be fair, my mommy issues
are another animal inside me.
A whole forest I return to.
I return there now. You
are alive and so am I
and so are the trees you watched
from our sliding glass door
chewing peanuts after a long
day at work. What was it like
coming home to us? I can't stop
asking. An owl landed on my fence
in Colorado at the end of a year
where I felt the most alone
I have ever felt. I failed at money
and career and love and still
someone new loves me
and I keep going without credit
or savings or a backup plan.
It is so hard to trust anything.
Where are you? We are both
mountains. In mountains.
Of mountains. A whole ancestry
of want in the sky.

Inside Me

inside me there is an old man with an old gray curly beard and the old man smokes cigarettes and sits in a big green recliner after work with a wedge pillow wedged against his low back he does not drink now but he will he will drink again and sometimes he will quit smoking and feel proud for all the long days of work for the children in the house for the nights early in bed for the wife even though she is on the couch

today he is just old and gray and the curls of his beard and the curls of his long brown and gray hair stick out and around like there's always a storm coming always a lightening strike just downstream just between that canyon and this old man sitting on a red canoe inside me or a forest green recliner the old man sits and sighs a Merit cigarette hangs from the corner of his mouth his teeth gently grasping to pull smoke in then let it out

the mountain man puffs and puffs and the puffs he takes are almost Appalachian and now he is fishing and now he is lifting the splintered wooden handles of the blue wheelbarrow and today it feels good to lift the blue metal and push it forward his belly pulled in to support his busted spine his hunger a fire inside his thirst larger than America

the old man inside me inhales deeply and then inhales again and the blue wheelbarrow winds along the back of the gray house past the stacked rocks and boulders to close off the end of the driveway so the cars his wife and daughter will drive don't go *willy nilly* into the mountain they need a barrier a boundary something he can make with materials at hand and he rounds the end of the stacked stones and wheels the wood toward the back sliding glass door to the basement there where dreams were once young and there is no room for that dream here or anymore so the old man inside me spits out the butt and stabs it with his tan cowboy boots grunts as his wrinkled and calloused hands toss two logs of earlier-axed oak up and out of the blue metal onto the red brick hearth by the dark black woodstove in the damp and cool basement where dreams once lived

he is working on Sunday always working and when he is done he is always standing he stands and looks out across the yellow and orange leaves of the not yet wintering Blue Ridge canopy and wonders if once again he'll be a hot-tempered drunk or if he'll finally be happy here with the quiet heart of a man who put his dreams into the woodstove into his work into the thing he is supposed to do or if one day he will walk around those stacked stones to the gravel driveway on Blue Ridge Mountain Road and start his old white work van walled with keys for those left stranded without them or with keys locked inside or maybe he'll open the black truck's door and toss a few things in the back maybe his guitar yes that's it one day the old man inside me will take his guitar and a pen and paper lots of coffee and Miller Lite and Merit cigarettes and tight Levi's and tan cowboy boots and carry himself like a prophet from one season of his life to the next

I feel him breathing in my blood it feels like smoke and a longing so deep I sense the desire the human desire the longing of war and one day he just starts singing and I think *that's it* the old man has walked off he sings a song he wrote for me which was really a song for love which is desire which is a blue mountain we'll never be able to leave no matter how far we let the tires burn the road the wood burn the stove there he is inside me singing what a surprise when I realize it's not a song but a sob

When the Heart is Heavy

Skin the sweet potatoes
Leave some skin for texture
Chop thick slices of shallots
Dice the garlic in uneven chunks
Toss in olive oil and generous
fingerfuls of salt and pepper
Rub the roots until they shine
Smear the rest across your skin
Roast
Wash the dishes
Turn off the music
Let the day slow-cook
despite the need
to drown out the noise
the daily injustices
Hear the dog ring the bells
on the back door
Let him out even though
he's just bored with your domesticity
your shuffling around
that doesn't involve him today
Dry your hands and stand
by the window
Your small fenced yard
and your four dogs sniffing
at the garage door
Their daily routine
in anticipation of the more
fun human home to play
See the chickens in their city
coop peck at insects
and kitchen scraps
They sense you by the door
Begin slow-clucks
squawks for attention
Hungry begs for more space
under the cold day to spread wings

and forage for something more
than this
To scratch at the dirt
and be covered in it

New Year's Day

the sun that morning blinded you at our kitchen table that up against the
window faced the dying tree beside the house our raised garden bed tilled over
for winter the neighbor's crumbling side porch and a too-bright day

I sat alone on weekday mornings when you were at work and meandered
through my early hours   sipped coffee alone fed tiny oats from my breakfast
bowl to our dogs oh I think I was lucky I trusted because time was your gift to
me then

sun warmed my face through the window as I watched the Northern Cardinals
feed their babies against the same post-sunrise Virginia sky I'd always known
and it was New Year's day after just a few years of us it felt special or new or
something

our schedules rarely allowed for such sweet long mornings together but
together we woke late and you wandered down to the kitchen and I stayed in
bed wished you had turned over in the lazy light and touched me woken me
with your hands I'd known for what then seemed so long

at the table I forgot my desire like I always did or pretended to do and you sat
beside me said the noon sun was too much for your eyes asked if we could eat
on the couch instead and I thought *this is it we are so different she doesn't love
light like I do*

I waited for you to read my face and agree or say what baby? and open the door
to everything I never said or stopped saying so as not to be too much too much
pressure should I have submitted then to our differences a poet who sat in the
sun blinded but happy

who loves the metaphor of the heart wanted you to toss all your guns into
the Atlantic and you the future cop Navy vet woman I thought loved me who
perhaps faked loving poetry but did distrust the heart as nothing more than a
muscle that pumps blood ventricle and vena cava

you all science and logic and quiet and accept you my house of mysterious
compartments me all heart and thrust all want want want I took a breath
another bite resolved again to finally take my mother's advice think before I

speak

I looked out our window at the day then back to you and squinted I couldn't
see your face my eyes struggled against the light *it is too bright here* I said and
you leaned in and smiled as we moved to the couch and from there I forgot
what I wanted

Dreamwork or Love

Your lover breaks up with you
in a dream because you can't keep
the sheets kicking like you used to
and you wake at the pink light of dawn
over a mountain that is not home.
Your lover is home in the city asleep
with your dogs and your sheets that smell
of so many years together no matter
how vigorously you wash them.
She wears her old blue sweatpants.
Her breath is as it always is
at dawn. You are hours away
making art and she is caring
for everything else. In the dream
you thought the two of you finally
found that spark again. But she pulled
back into the dark sticky matter
of imagination. You sat naked
on the bed and it was also a kitchen.
She was into you—one hand on your inner
thigh, fingers barely tempting neglected lips,
and distracted. You ruin the moment with talk
like therapy so she calls her Navy friend
to come pick her up. *Let's hang out* she says
and there he is with a bottle of whiskey.
You reach for her, swear you'll shut
your mouth, but now you're at brunch
without money and there are dogs
tied up across the street. They're hungry
and lunging and about pull away
from their leashes.

Seven Years

where did the night go   our days so full   of nothing   so long   our bed
became a place to nod off early with the dogs   you were my center   my
pillar   my sturdy cement foundation   what difference did it make what we
did   to live   I decided to keep loving you when you decided to be a cop   in
the year of bad cops and dead people who shouldn't be dead   I said what
better woman lesbian liberal well-read person in uniform than you   so I kept
loving you even though   I knew you might finger the trigger and everything
I'd read to you about privilege in that second wouldn't matter   it would be
you or them   maybe no one will ever die by your hands   the same hands
I craved as our eyelids won every goddamn night   what causes pain   the
nonexistent scenarios I dreamed up   the nonexistent future consoling your
guilt for the body that dropped   the nonexistent nights spent cleaning your
shit after surviving a shot   what brings lust back   the cuffs dangling from
your belt   the excitement of riding along as you repeat codes   10-4   27-8
10-99   watching you be hard   my secret wish that you were harder   took
me harder   tossed me to the ground   I wanted you to cuff me in bed   play
good cop bad cop   it's true   it's true I was so bored I waited for tragedy   it's
true that's why I stayed   why I said I'd support you no matter who you shot
it's true when you quit I wondered what now   how will we find tension again
I craved danger   never said it   I stuck to my desk to our home our dogs
and the stove   you craved a different danger   a straight woman   her body
some law you could trust

For More

How comfortable I became. How easy my lack of intimacy, how quick each goodnight kiss, how habitual my rolling over away from her preferred away, how for granted I took her heavy hand on my hip. Love was good, wasn't it? There was something more I wanted and did not name, another dimension caught in my throat. Even when I knew my body couldn't take it anymore— anticipation a sharp scent in the air before snow—even when I begged her with subtle shifts of my pelvis—her soft belly against my lower back—to break the cycle of easier sleep, even when my pulse felt it might freeze unless I mustered the courage to travel my own hand from its easy rest at her oblique to the wet season between her heavy thighs, even when that habit of love and partnership, that *this is just how old love is* my only hold on faith, even when I worried if comfort of home, my steady elixir, might spoil if what had settled was not stirred—I still turned to her after hearing those deeper breaths of sleep, let my fingers linger over the birthmark I swore was growing and she swore was always that size and shade, and for a moment it was there where I remembered I had nothing to hold onto. It was there I chose to stay, despite. Stay. Nothing to hold onto. Only my lonely body and all her quiet needs floating around the room lost in space. Oh my heart's deep river, remember her now, remember my sharp tugs beneath the skin for more. Remember how wise you thought you were. How dumb, and alone.

After the Move

I was new and raw
didn't know the land
on daily walks thousands
of hand-sized grasshoppers
jumped and scattered some
slipped into the space
between my foot and sandal
I didn't stop felt the stick
and smash and crunch
of fat bodies under my arch
at dawn I'd let out the dogs
watch them piss on stubby desert
trees as families of prairie dogs
scampered into their holes
herds and herds huddled
on desert dust mounds
little surprising barks
their fear of strangers
on once deserted land stark
open-mouthed
I stumbled forward like this
many weeks with no purpose
drowsy and pulled into so much
sky dry tan earth of everything
sharp high desert plants and seeds
stuck to my skin
needles and thistles scratched
my toes still too stubborn
to ditch my east coast sandals
locals said wear boots
watch for rattlers
none yet in those early days
so I pretended like I always do
that I wasn't afraid
I did see my first black widow
then a second then too many
to count and I knew my girlfriend

played with tarantulas in her backyard
like many New Mexican children
rode stubborn horses bareback
before she could fix her own meal
I sat on one of her mother's old beasts
for just a few short trots around
the corral cried hard and fast
when she bucked
how easy to forget
which heel to dig
which rein to pull
who am I now
asked over and over I still
ask now that I'm gone
I followed that love
to her home then away
then alone again those mountains
around me were not the Blue Ridge
but from a distance as I drove
north followed the Sangre de Cristos
until they were just the Rockies
to another after yes from that distance
I really couldn't tell the difference

Who Lives and Who Dies

we bought a pregnant goat   spent the first days as close to her   as she'd let
us   tried to pet her wiry fur   coaxed her with apples   bright green alfalfa
kept her in a large kennel near the trailer   plenty of shaved cedar   she never
slept on   we waited for her to learn our safe scents   comfort instead of threat
read up on birthing   health   milk   three days in we heard our first coyote
pack   they circled the yard   called to each other   laughed like angry hyenas
you grabbed your gun   ran to the fence   all respond and react   I let the
dogs out to growl into the dark   we couldn't see them wholly   but caught
quick glimpses of golden eyes circling the yard   I begged you not to shoot
remembering books I'd read about predators   how desperately our ecosystems
need them   how they will multiply   no matter how many ranchers   or
amateur hobby farmers try to kill them off   our shy girl paced in the kennel
squatted every few minutes dumping buckets of piss onto the ground   skin
tight   every strand of hair on my body   a million pumping hearts awake   like
first fear   this   my early lesson of humans   our relationship with stock   how
we choose   tame   pretend to protect   a more primal creature's prey

Praise Song

last night at dusk while I was at work and the dogs were chasing mice barking at horses it must have scurried by the fence or under the old brown farm truck and no one saw it happen then my lover drove them home and the car filled with a smell like chemical pesticide gasoline and I came home to find her close to tears scrubbing the smelliest one for the third time in the tub sniffing her fur trying to figure it out *what could it be* she asked *her eyes are burning what did they get into did someone spray their fields tonight* then her mother texted to say she saw a skunk scurrying around the horse corral and oh how we laughed phones in our hands ready to call poison control so back to the tub we went for the right combination of peroxide baking soda dish soap essential oil oh praise that skunk who sprayed all four dogs who lifted its tail and let loose its defense against their hungry jaws and oh hell praise too the smell lingering for weeks in their shiny coats the smell stuck to our tub our couch our sheets yes praise all the stench that won't wash out praise the small dark crevices we sniff toward like hungry animals on the hunt for what we can't see

In Defense

this morning as we milked our goat   I yelled at you with rage I thought
reserved   for family   or myself   this after your simple reminder   tinged
with annoyance to keep the milking tools sanitary   how quick the grit of my
jaw   grind of my teeth   shot look back as if you   killed one of our dogs
snap of my voice like the nagging wife   I promised you I'd never be   when
rage wins I am not human   in defense I am more animal than ever   not
devoted canine or shy milking goat   more mother grizzly protecting some
inner   vulnerable cub   you held the kid in your lap   his eyes grew heavy
and soft   I hobbled momma's hoof to the milking stand you built from scrap
wood   cleaned her udder the way you explained with patience   after doing
all the research   attached the milker you bought to her teat   started the
hand pump   she kicked   and the kid nodded off in your arms   the air
softened as we marveled   at the gallon of milk made in mere minutes   while
momma munched her grain   later I am alone   you are at work   goats asleep
in their little barn   yes   you built that too   it's true I help   I hand you
tools   help place bricks once you share your blueprints   I'd like to say that
before I loved you I was never afraid   that I was happy drinking wine alone
in my apartments eating whole pizzas   but rage is a kind of grip   I'm scared
of everything   mostly loss   every time I leave home   now that we've moved
to the country   I drive off   imagine the house burns to the ground with our
four dogs kenneled inside   or   while home alone   lazy pups draped over my
thighs   I see your long drive over the mountain in a snowstorm   picture a
truck losing it on the ice   I can smell the searing skin   see your face trapped
beneath a crushed car frame   what I mean is I'm sorry   I love you   never
leave

After the Breakup

so all my days have added up to this   I look at my body and see myself as
flesh   as something like love   as something like a life carried by pain   that
fading scar on my leg looks like the letter *E*   I carved it   *EDNOS*   during
one of many long and lonely nights with less hope a lot of cheap wine   a whole
pizza down the hatch   then a mess in the toilet   my notebooks scribbled full
how badly I wanted to be more   always more   hardly legible   a twenty-
something's hunger drawn   in blood on the page   did I know then   the only
way was through   because oh how I drenched myself like a baptism in all the
pain no one outside me could hold   and here I am again alone   afraid of who
I might meet   inside the dark hall of myself   so what does the body carry
now   a newly renovated home I no longer own   600 fence posts I drove and
banged into the ground under the hot desert sun   two goats I lured behind
that fence   who   I imagine still bleat for my hands at dawn   a life I thought
was mine where her new love lives   a relationship now only a dream I keep
waking up to   sweaty in the dark   legs covered in stretch marks   purple
veins   so many years on my feet   a thirst like a throb coming into my own
desire unmuted   tenacity like a canyon the river comes through   a woman
without a home   a woman who was asked without words to leave her home
a woman's body a heartbreak   sobbing all over her new city   crying for a love
lost a new love brought in and lost too   all the old buildings knocked down
around me   gentrification next door at my door all the bodies gone   new
bodies wiped clean   bodies bodies all the bodies dying and little old me   the
same young girl begging for a love I fear doesn't exist   no I know now   the
love I want   is not outside   I understand now why so many wanderers
without homes walk around full scream in public   stories so loud in our hearts
incessant thumps against each wall of the body   how can anyone survive this
I keep asking   and I smile at a stranger   every cell open   hungry and sharp
I soften my gaze   look at her and mean it   oh stranger my broken body wants
you   wants something I cannot name   so many books open and face-down
on my chest   so we talk about something   more than the weather   *what else
is living for*   she asks me   and my body is water   instantly river

Away

Yes, it's true. I left
what was broken, what wasn't mine.
That gray house with all the windows.
The farmhouse kitchen table she built for us.
The homemade stain we made to darken the young
raw wood. It soaked up all the liquid in our hands.
When she turned toward her next lover, so fast,
I sat dumfounded in my new, freshly painted home.
I swallowed something hard and quick so I could leave.
The coyotes circled the open ranchlands, the high desert
barely beginning to settle dry in my bones
as home. The mountains in every direction
pulled at my gut. All the howling
in the sky. Blue that was not quite
blue enough. Was that life a dream?
Are all the places I think are home
dream, too? I half-dressed myself
in myself every day. I walked around homeless
in a home I begged for. In front of a person I now know
was an art I failed to mold. Her body a home
I tried to call into. I was half myself and maybe
it was never the hungry coyotes
but the whole of my bloodstream howling.
When I drove away, I stopped three times
on the long gravel driveway and dry-heaved
two weeks of stress bile from my belly onto the red dirt
and dust. I looked back at her, smoking on our steps.
She watched me, but did not come.
Home was not home. The birds called me away
from the high desert plains. Pushed against wind
and I followed. Thank god I followed.

Burn It Down

Burn your old life and go home, Tara. There's no more love in that loveless house. No walls left to paint shades of gray and blue, no lover to make any trim and decorative decisions with, and for. She's gone, even though she stays, puts away her memory of you, all your heavy stories, your heavy dripping heart, your heavy thrust toward the nothing in your bed. Burn your photos and birthday cards, Tara. The ones you're holding onto for no reason except to remember her shaky cursive writing, her trite salutations nothing like a poem, nothing like the words you want from lovers now. (What do you want from all these lovers now?) Burn the dog hair and the dust, burn the long dirt road that flooded a thick new river during August's short rainy season—the desert suddenly an ocean around the house you could never quite step into, wholly. Burn it all, Tara. It was never yours and you knew it then. That knowing a quiet screaming between the deep bones of your wide and flexible hips. Every time you turned the gold key on the flimsy double-wide back door, the door already bent and banged up from all that wild wind—every time, oh how many goddamn times you opened it and let it get away—a slam against the cheap siding, a persistent dent on the side of your new house, waking the dogs from their quiet slumbers in all the corners you didn't have time to fill. Set that old story of a life on fire. The hidden headlights between your thighs point north and forward and all around. They light up something green and electric—like heart, like an internal spring, something like a sky lit by wet wet earth. There's still light there. Let it out. Let your wanting flame the old story, let it illuminate something bare, pulse a glow on the whole naked skin of your desire—this creature growing out of the lie you finally let go of. Burn it to let it go. Stop dragging around a dead goat wrapped in barbed wire—double and triple wrapped around your useless hands—her dried up udders painting a sad trail in the red dirt behind you. All those fucking empty mason jars you filled and cleaned, filled and cleaned? Turn melted glass into something useful. Into art. Burn the body. Bury her, and go. This was not home. Those nights under the southwestern sky were not yours to keep. Stories are lies I tell, desperate. As if truth were something we could hold onto, as if truth were identity, or love, or the body we were lucky enough to let in our bed for some short, or long time. All time is short. All of this is long. And of course story is everything. And of course everything matters. The sky and burning, the corpses and hot glass turned to dust in your open open hands. No one around for miles and miles and miles except an old lover inside turning toward another, the dead dogs still alive and you, the pitch black, all those millions of stars not yet dead to you, but not alive. Not at all. Burn and rise, Tara. There's no love here. No love at all. Just a story. Ash and sky. A road to follow. A new bed. A body yours and only yours. These hungry thighs opening and closing. And opening.

Declaration

I will begin the meal
without a plan. Brown
butter and onions. Add
garlic too soon, watch it
crisp. Massage a bloody loin
with bare hands. Wait
for clarity of intention.
Press salt into its flesh
and thrust the ruminant
into my hot iron pan.
What a surprise
to find patience here.
In slow preparation
after a youth spent sped up
and afraid of long hours
doing anything, especially
at a stove. This is service
to my body. To love. To
home. Domesticity
can be radical.
Can be lesbian.
These are good ways
to stick it to the man:
cook food, love
women, enjoy
staying home.
Clarity is simple:
a quick sear,
the thick drizzle
of juice from what's
here. A simple space
between life and food.
I will no longer deny
the belly's call for fat
and flesh. I will love
this body because she
is hungry and she

is mine. I am animal
like any other.

Stories I Told

We were happy and I was broken and a little unhinged so I needed her she was an anchor a steel tool dropped to the bottom of my ocean she was my night watch on the destroyer of me out at sea she protected me and at some point in the beginning of us I decided I needed protecting even though every part of me said go especially after I convinced her to get drunk again and again on weeknights that red porch our place to loosen up touch just a little then head to the bedroom her phone left there ringing ringing at 4am to call in for duty her officer or whatever you call them I never learned the words on his way to her house and us naked and illegal in her bed I was a dangerous thing I was in need of a home and something practical steady someone who cared about her boss and the laws against bodies but after I while I was happy wasn't I I was in bed with the warm light on and the dogs at our feet and around the bed so many dogs and she was a back turned toward me and we ate and got fat happy and I didn't care how little we made love anymore because I was home I was safe she saved me and I was tired and she was tired and her quiet fixed me I was a thing to fix I was a thing and I loved it all four dogs and the home we stopped inviting people to because dogs and hair everywhere and then the move to New Mexico and how much I pushed I wanted it didn't I and didn't she too want to leave the coast leave my home leave Virginia and the wet air and the weight there all the industry in the skyline I loved the 400 square-foot trailer we had to live in and I was thankful for her judgmental rural doomsday prepper conspiracy theory family so the 1970s wood paneling was fine and I cleaned and stacked our boxes until there was no more room and it looked like a home as we looked for our next home oh I loved the leaks and the tar roof and the tires on the roof holding it all down from the wind and the goat she got me she always gave me what I wanted every tangible thing so I didn't mind the hum in my body between my thighs all the screaming there I loved the milk jars and the sink filled with glass jars and dog bowls and so many things to clean I wanted to live in the country so far away from life and people and my people and the house we bought was my idea wasn't it even though I pointed out the mountain land I thought we agreed on over and over we ended up on 10 acres south and east of everything except her next lover and by then we'd been together so long I tricked myself into wanting it all the 6 different shades of gray paint on the new walls the placement of the goat barn the wrong kind of gravel that sunk into the red mud I knew gravel I grew up on gravel but still she didn't listen because I let her think I knew nothing and I let her tell me with her body I was too much I didn't want to pack up and leave I didn't want every single queer body I met in Albuquerque at work I didn't hate dog sports I didn't hate watching her play dog sports for like 48 hours straight on our only days off together I didn't hate the woman she met that loved dog sports and training as much as she did I didn't hate the idea to turn the back acres into a Dock Dogs pool I didn't think dogs jumping into pools for ribbons was boring I wanted it all anything to keep her I didn't think there was something wrong with me did I why else did I stay did I support her career change a deputy sheriff in a state that arrested every brown person that crossed the border and killed a homeless man simply sitting alone in nature of nature I wanted it all I would have supported her no matter who she shot I even begged her back as I packed up a rental van and left while she married a woman who loved to train too and now the field where my art shack would live and the place I walked the goats to milk every day is a dog training business and didn't I see it coming I was happy I was in love I was broken she was perfect what a story what a fantastic lie the house the gray walls the little robot vacuum trying to keep everything clean the farmhouse table a place to sit and eat together without heads down on our phones

Exercise in Which a Poet in Heartbreak Finds Herself in a Writing Class with Fiction Writers and Doesn't Leave, Rebels a Little, Learns to Put Characters Under Pressure

I: write a scene, something new, just one character doing something

She sat by the gold Chevy Blazer. She sat on a bucket, overturned. Her body was cloaked from wrists to ankles in blue coveralls she wore in the Navy on the USS Austin. The bucket was overturned on the dusty New Mexico dirt. The sky was open around her in a way that made direction feel infinite. She was bent over. She was thinking and tinkering at the same time. The gold Chevy Blazer, made in the year 2000, had been jacked up. She had jacked up the front half of the Gold Blazer. The car was half-lifted and held. Her tools surrounded her. Her tools fanned out, misplaced and haphazard, on the dusty red dirt. Socket wrenches and drills and a bright neon green Ryobi bag of tools. The bright green Ryobi bag of tools was unorganized. Tubes of sticky black grease laid in the bag, open, oozing. She wore blue nitrile gloves and didn't care that the tools were unorganized. All her tools and unwound twine tangled with tubes of oozing grease. Hammers and crow bars in the dirt. A light plugged in 100 feet behind her in the busted and windblown shed. The desert was wind. Her girlfriend held the light. Talked. Her girlfriend talked to her while she loosened the bolts around the tire, one by one. Her strength was in her arms. Her strength was in what she knew. Her girlfriend passed her tools. Sometimes she passed the wrong tools. They laughed. Nothing much was ever at stake. Nothing there was under pressure, except the tires. The tires were under pressure, but they weren't broken. It was the rods that held it all together. The tie rods and maybe the axles. The girlfriend doesn't remember. The girlfriend isn't the girlfriend anymore. But when the girlfriend drove the year 2000 gold Chevy Blazer something clunked. Something always clunked. The girlfriend always asked her to fix the something that always clunked. She always fixed it: the car, the clunking, the girlfriend. She sat on the overturned bucket in the dry and dusty New Mexico dirt and fixed the 2000 gold Chevy Blazer. She always fixed it. The girlfriend handed her tools. The girlfriend played music, held the light, balanced the light in a safe place when she was bored and went inside to get beer or wine or whiskey. The girlfriend brought her beer. She drank the beer, but when she was focused on fixing things she was focused on fixing things. She focused on fixing things and didn't drink the beer until the task was done. The task was done. But the task was never done. Inside, the girlfriend peed, got beer, pet the dogs. She fixed the car. The girlfriend made dinner while she fixed things.

II: put that character under internal pressure

She sits on the overturned bucket by the Blazer, fixing it for her girlfriend. Fixing her girlfriend. She wants to be training their dogs. She always wants to be training the dogs. And she wants to be in Iceland where she was many years ago. In Iceland she found joy and sex and freedom for the first time after boot camp and a-school. Anywhere but here, she wants. She wants to be back on the USS Austin with her ex and in Iceland with her other ex and the American base and all that comes with American bases. She wants to be there with her ex because her ex was dangerous and never really wanted her so it was a game. Her ex was a game and her girlfriend is not. Her girlfriend wants everything from her and she feels it. This makes everything hard but she doesn't show it. Everything is hard and she does not want to be wanted but when asked she says everything is great of course. I love you of course. This home is our home of course. She doesn't have to hide her everything is wrong because she never really shows anything she wants or feels on the outside, until it bursts. Under pressure. On the outside, she can fix things. On the outside, she can sit on the bucket and let her girlfriend who wants everything from her pass her tools and play Tegan and Sara and bring her beer and check on the dogs and make food and yes they laugh together because it is good on the outside or it used to be but on the inside it is years of this and she is bored. On the inside she is bored or complacent and fine of course. She wants her ex because she doesn't know what else to want because imagining a better future together or alone would show too much on the outside and besides her ex was straight so it was a game. Her ex was straight and they were on a ship at sea and they hid in the little gray crevices on the USS Austin together and fucked like their lives were at stake because they were, they were out at sea. They were out at sea and *don't ask don't tell* and everything was dangerous. Everything was dangerous as they floated around the horn of Africa and fixed the airwaves, the high frequency waves and the ultra high frequency waves and she fixed it all. She fixed it all every time it went down so the USS Austin could carry all the bodies not asking and not telling communicating across high and very and ultra high frequencies so pirate ships could get blasted at night. Pirate ships got blasted at night and they slept in little bunks tucked in tight like little births. Like little births they were bodies tucked in at sea wanting each other all of it dangerous. Her ex was dangerous because her ex was straight and eventually slept with men on the ship while they all floated out at sea. Her ex eventually slept with men on the ship and even though it broke her she didn't let it show she moved on and bought a yellow house without her ex and all this she remembered as she fixed the 2000 gold Chevy Blazer and her current girlfriend who is not dangerous and wants everything from her stands beside her and hands her tools and beer and tells her everything, all the thoughts in her head and all her love for her too, so obvious of course. Her girlfriend who is not dangerous or dramatic, though everything she feels is drama to her why does she have to feel so much and be so of course. Her girlfriend who is drama but does not involve her in drama or danger is safe and safely hands her tools and plays the same music they always listen to and does not hide anything so nothing is mysterious or erotic anymore and she fixes the Blazer and everything here is *tell* instead of *don't tell* instead of *let me figure it out with my body in a dark dangerous crevice.* She fixes the Blazer and it brings her pleasure. Her hands here on oiled tools and parts bring her pleasure and satisfaction but her body wants to be in charge of something unsafe again. Her body wants to be in charge of something unsafe again but now she wants to wear a bodysuit made of jute and let a dog bite her for sport because when the dog bites her she is alive and in danger but in control. She thinks of this as she fixes the car and her girlfriend, beautiful and poetic and full of something she no longer enjoys, does the same things she always does and fills the air with her talk and her wanting. She fixes the car. She focuses there. She thinks of her ex girlfriend and her current girlfriend and how much it would hurt if she makes her leave this house and this unfixable 2000 gold Chevy Blazer. She thinks of how much it would hurt to make her leave. She thinks of the woman 20 miles away training dogs, her blonde body straight woman body her perfect body her next danger. She thinks of her and she wants it all.

III: *put external pressure on your character, make something happen on the outside*

There was never much pressure here. Or, was there always pressure here. The tire wasn't at stake, it would never explode, even though her girlfriend always asked her dumb questions about air in tires. Her girlfriend always asked her dumb questions about air in tires and what makes a person explode. No, a tire. What makes a tire explode. She thought she might explode because her girlfriend always asked dumb questions. She didn't always think the girlfriend asked dumb questions. 7 years ago, when the girlfriend was into her like an art project, the questions she asked were mysterious. Her girlfriend was a poem was a witch was art and mysterious. The questions her girlfriend asked 7 years ago were beautiful and mysterious and art and her darkness then turned her on. 7 years ago her girlfriend turned her on because she was surprisingly interested in her boring and bland Navy lifestyle and because 7 years ago her girlfriend was art and something wild like unbrushed hair something she never had on a ship out at sea and because 7 years ago her girlfriend listened to her answers and pretended to care enough to help and learn something new. 7 years ago her girlfriend wore her extra pair of Navy blue coveralls from the USS Oscar Austin and they sat on overturned buckets beside each other and for a moment her girlfriend was dangerous because she was art. 7 years ago she sat on an overturned bucket beside her in the dim light of the garage in Virginia. In the dim light of the garage in Virginia they both sat on buckets and drank beer and listened to Tegan and Sara songs for only the first and second and third times together. They listened to so many lesbian songs together and everything was new it was all pressure their bodies sat beside each other on overturned buckets with beers in both hands and she taught her girlfriend who did not ask dumb questions then about the tools in her hand. The tools in their hands. 7 years ago her girlfriend held tools in her hand and jacked up the 2000 gold Chevy Blazer with her until the back end tilted back and the small garage filled with their wanting and grease on their faces. 7 years ago they both wore blue nitrile gloves and no one cared about organization in the tool bag and she didn't know if they'd last long but she wanted her girlfriend's body beneath her discontinued Navy blue coveralls. She wanted her then new girlfriend's body beneath the discontinued Navy blue coveralls and her new girlfriend talked and asked questions but it was hot pressure then no pressure to fix anything for the first time in so long the only pressure was to fuck of course. To fuck of course in the dim light of her bedroom later their bodies new and greased and full of questions and mechanics and art and of course a reverence for the other like difference was delicate and of course they fucked 7 years ago the yellow house still empty and new and her not dumb girlfriend hadn't moved in yet and the walls were tan like the New Mexico dirt they would eventually move toward inhabit then fall flat and bored together but here it was all bare and bursting with the pleasure of extreme difference and there was no pressure to go anywhere no pressure to move no pressure, no pressure at all.

Transformation

Swollen face. Tears
like hot glue. All these days
stuck wet to the skin. My life
is an arrow pointed at the dusk-blue
sky and the dusk-blue sky is an arrow
pointed back at me. A bird sings.
I say things that may not be true.
A man in an orange vest
jackhammers the hell
out of the concrete parking lot
outside my therapist's office as I sob.
He jackhammers the hell out of it.

Queer Girl

I have been the filthiest dirt the dirtiest dirt I have been queer like a cow pressing against a fence to taste what's kept from her I have pressed and pressed and rubbed my body all over everything corners and pillows and electric toothbrushes and a vibrating neck pillow my mother slept on and what's it like to have been born so queer the girl everyone said was pretty and bright until she talked or felt or told stories out loud or watched all the bodies in front of her for just a few moments too long or when she was in a hot tub with friends in fifth grade saying here press yourself here against the jets yes like that until we all laughed and came and I wonder still if they thank the tub and our orgasms together still so many women who don't until their twenties or thirties or worse and yes I showed my friends how to come before I knew what the word orgasm was before I knew women should be ashamed of spreading their legs or pressing against anything on their own time or laughing with other young girls god forbid we found something together where are they now where are you young girls sing this song with me you were queer did you know that we found something together and now I know there is no word still for our better floods the flashed arroyos the dirty fingernails of our childhood pressed between the parts we still struggle to find the right words for labia mons pubis inner and outer and fatty sticky parts the scent now rising from my chair my legs open my arroyo still wet and muddy from a morning with my girlfriend her body a light I turned to and no I do not care that her body as light may be cliché to you fuck your rules fuck your right or wrong words for poems for sex the way we baby everything up with white powders and the talc that destroyed my grandmother's ovaries her mother convincing her to powder her panties every single day of her life so only like a baby down there only like a powder like something white and so clean it kills I hate being too clean give me the stink the old world wine with grit in the glass and dirt on the tongue let me place my tongue on everything let me learn audacity finally let my tongue on the dirt of me press shame out of everything out of you out of you a sweat no scent can hide a leather hide a dank dank earth a core we haven't found yet my lesbian fingernails clipped down to pink skin so I can take my unwashed hand and discover all the darkest filthiest parts of myself is this uncomfortable and a little wrong a little unsanitary a bit in need of something that kills to wipe it up keep your clean things your white wipes and white powders and clean diets out of every part of me do you understand that even now I still hate myself like everything normative has told me to do you understand how badly I want to go back to the tub with those girls and grab their hands run free naked and covered in suds and every stank and dank liquid coming coming out of us go ahead tell me this is gratuitous let me spill open and quiet the very puritan ways of you let me spread my queer legs all over the language meant to keep me from everything let me tell you this keeps us from everything

Blueberry Syrup

for Mom

On days like this on Wednesdays when office workers send emails with various camels in varying sexual positions the phrase *Happy Hump Day!* typed over said humping—

On days like this when I'm home at my desk and for once thankful for the courage to not take any office job to not resign to shoulds to not *grow up* make my life a thing and not a life something for your comfort to not take a job where I may find myself rolling my eyes like a teenager at my other desk neighbor and his louder than anyone ever black coffee slurping whole hours of blowing into the magic mug of awake slurp blow slurp blow sigh grunt every goddamn morning for over an hour—

On days like this I could assimilate to survive it send my own cheesy ass email memes instant message said slurpy desk neighbor instead of turning toward his slouched shoulders touching the round of his posture gently tugging out his ear buds disrupting the daze of the blue blue light from three computer screens pushed together like a theater a performance of things to do at once the lies we tell ourselves *I work best under immense stress* and *oh I'm a great multitasker*—

On days like this when I live in sweatpants forget how to bathe respond to a few student emails with more ease than usual *sure you can have a few more days* I say *take care of yourself first* because I am too I ignore grading a happy refusal to feel bad about it meander through books write long run-on sentences like my students do when drafting pause to cuddle my dogs make bread press my fists into dough knead it need it stare out the window at the dogwood trees coming into bloom—

On days like this I contemplate home and Virginia how sand and mountain and farm and city of first colonies city of first slave ships city and swamps of so much early slaughter now prisons filled with black and brown bodies who don't get away with the kinds of crimes I've committed the things and days I have stolen the risks taken on long drives almost blacked out my young life a swerve through green green mountain roads and bright gray city streets all this in my body and all this I have a little time to think on and not doubt at least not today—

On days like this when eleven French journalists are shot dead and there are hostages and again we wonder *Am I safe? What is safety? Am I next? This job this school this building these babies that bullshit war we're so privileged not to see, not really What else am I blind to? when will another gunman's anger which is just fear untethered let loose?* when again will we look around dumbfounded like we have over and over *say I just don't understand people those kinda people* or *well there's nothing we can do about that—*

On days like this when Assata Shakur posts an open letter from her safer life in Cuba after President Obama announced *renewed diplomatic ties* and she has to explain again word-for-word step-by-step what went down on the New Jersey Turnpike that day in 1973 the 5-0 and feds and most of this country that will never ever believe women not really especially not a black woman especially not a black woman in the Black Liberation Army all of us whether we know it or not still out for her blood out for blood we're all drenched in this blood (and I say go—escape from the jails and fuck all the establishments let's form all the liberation armies free every single body we can I'm done)—

On days like this when we know we must march for everything free and we know protests are now commonplace now normal as breakfast (what would a day without protest even look like?)—

On days like this when my little overbred blue pit bull with an under bite that forces her tongue out her mouth like taffy her knobby knees and aggression bred into her a six-week old energetic puppy left outside without shelter without nurture or touch those formative weeks where attachment is necessary taken as her little body was kicked and thrown across the yard yelled at spit on covered in shit and piss and she growls at me in her sleep unsure if it is today or yesterday unsure if she's ever really safe or if my hand petting her soft trembling dream-whine fur might shift grab her snout and squeeze I know when I look at her I know when we're snuggled hard she knows how to bite if she has to and not let go—

On days like this when it's all too much when I'm face down on the floor and yes there's that doubt that inner *what the fuck are you even doing with your life Tara get it together get a better degree or job join an activist group make more money get out of debt save some save something save someone besides yourself what on earth are all these words for when suffering is all around* when language feels like self-indulgence and not power not the ground for body and story you mostly believe in when I forget that writing and teaching without agenda or really any care that they learn to cite in the correct tedious format (it's all about ownership isn't it) when I forget that all I want is to sit in community speak write and heal together—

then my student the meth addict clean for just 6 months disappears from the classroom then my one native student who was writing about life on the res is gone too and the one whose grandfather was shot by a Mexican cartel member a recruit who was just a child like him who was then shot too and he cries in class we all witness in silence then another young brown man places a hand on his shoulder says *it's okay, man* and I know I know in the whole of my skin this is a classroom that matters this is what we're here for then my white student in the room the Army vet who suffers from PTSD and a whole life of resentment *can't be depressed and in the military* he said to me stays after complains about giving *those chatty Mexican kids too much room to share just personal shit that doesn't matter white people are shot too* and it's all so clearly connected all of us so heavy with *how* so we agree to disagree we shop we shoot up we turn on the reruns we drink until we puke and do it all again—

On days like this when I feel the weight of you mom all you suffered at the hands of men all they did and said about your body all the words around your body still all you gave up to make me   me this mess of a blue body too suffering and strong in a way I can't quite describe in a poem it's still abstract the body you put on me no image for this no metaphor between us on days like this I roll my eyes the way I used to and sigh as I practice the bs practice of gratitude and it works if only for a moment—

On days like this I remember your blueberry pancakes with blueberry syrup made each Christmas from a year of frozen blueberries that I'd like to say came from picking together but didn't like most things we ate they came from a box saved from leftover canned berries in the Jiffy muffin pre-made mix—

On days like this I remember home and food the good of it instead and those early Christmas mornings you showered us with more toys and games than we would ever find time to play despite never having money for it how we sat in our mountain of presents as dad walked around cigarette hanging from his teeth breathing hard to hold his judgment worried how spoiled we were who we might become how he picked up our trash and smiled when we showed him what he bought us even though we all knew you shopped and wrapped wrote his name on the tags and how after gifts you shifted to the kitchen got to work flipping cakes on the flat skillet pouring thawed Ziploc bags of blueberries into a Teflon sauce pot with cornstarch and sugar and I have to remember this I make myself remember you best as the one who taught me to taste as I go to not worry much about details though I do I worry so much as I feel things through I was only allowed to be there with you if I stirred and kept the bottom from burning and provide very specific thickening updates—

You burned the first few then piled a plate high so many pancakes for the four of us you'd make at least thirty and the house filled with sweet batter all our hunger this was my favorite part of Christmas one of the only gifts I remember in your mountains of gifts how your blueberry syrup congealed into a thickness I haven't yet seen replicated and when it was all ready the four of us sat in front of the television surrounded by so much stuff all gone now we'd eat at least ten a piece go back for seconds and thirds more milk to wash it all down—

on days like this when I know we're all dying we're going to drown or starve or be shot on this hot earth together but not quite together enough I wish instead we were some semblance of that family you tried to keep simple together drowning it all in syrup—

I wish my lips were sticky and blue—

on days like this all I want is to eat, have home back, say thank you

Let Us Live

Let us be big and heavy red wines, let us leave our thick legs on the glass. Let us drink and be drunk. Let us be hungry and want the skin of every human wet against our lips, our tongues wild and untamed, salt-thirsty. Let us eat the rich meats and thick, buttery sauces, let us be the stinky cheese, the aged and blue, the soft, delicious and dangerous. Let us buy on impulse and never pay the bills—like a coven let us just live in the red and meditate, content as the money squirms. Let us be excess—a spare tire over tight jeans, a crop top above a soft middle, a braless summer day. Let's walk tall in our contradictions—our strides can swing or swagger, our hearts can burn in rage and joy in one day. Let our children be chubby and loud—oh let us be those chunky cheeks again—let's take off our shirts and splash in the mud, fall on our fat asses and be glad in it.

Blue Body Hungry for Origin or Certainty

Born blue. Not without breath. Blue as mountain. Blue as soul. Something deep and unknowable. Am I savior for the broken hearts I hunger for? Am I the broken heart I hunger for? Savior only for myself? Broken bodies made me. I was broken. I don't believe in broken. Is there such thing as whole, as holy, really? Watch the birds fly in unison. As one. A cluster rises from a dying shrub. The desert I left behind. The open field. The open. Blue New Mexico sky. What beckoned me. The teal of rough turquoise before polish, the sky here, home now, between sunshine and storm.

Everything was orange, was red dirt and dust. A wind I could never win. The body knew she was an anchor in a dried-up sea she was heavy on the floor her tether tossed up and out to no one the body knew she was barely living save her breath and the breath of the body beside her and oh how she wanted oh how she wanted everything all the hands inside her the body knew she was body and also no body at all she was hunger without container she was thirst without faucet she was a scream without a mouth oh who was she then but a body beside a body rolled over and away from her always

dear me five years ago

you had no idea
what was coming
remember this
and bow to it all

The wind in the trees—the green shade trees, the Virginia mountain trees, the tiny New Mexico junipers and piñons and tall yellow aspens and persistent pines and windblown Colorado cottonwoods—all are god to me, the cotton stuck to my sweaty face now god and this tired day in tears is god too and all my mistakes, the lives I've lived and refuse to regret are god, which is art, which is poetry, the ultimate made thing, the call *to make*—our divine attention to everything we can possibly see beyond ourselves. Our songs in language, the deep night of image and sound, how what we don't know and still move toward can open every pore. And god too is just the perfect hand inside the perfect deeper garden between the thighs—her perfect hand inside mine and our mouths open as the wind blows the trees as the poem crescendos between us and begs the perfect question, no answer, only question, only leaves in the breeze, only simultaneous bodies lips on lips on lips on lips—I live for lips for this kind of deep, the holy deep, the holy *slow down please,* so holy I lose the borders between us.

Remind me how to love it all, how to embody what I say is mine, this deep blue love for body all bodies and skin, the round and thin, small and tall, the way clothes fit us all, the muscles and the wrinkles and the scars the hip bones and collarbones and soft belly fat, the way we walk and stand, how we lean into one hip while we wait in lines to avoid the core of ourselves, the spines and deep bellies and pelvises that hold us up if we let them, what's under the ridiculous fabrics, what's under us all, how breasts perk and fall, what flaccid dicks look like as they swaddle the seams of pants.

I want to see it all.

I want the story of your body, how you first opened your legs to another, what was safe. Who wasn't. Who hurt you. Who have you hurt. Yes, I want this. Fuck the weather. Give me our grief, the way your body holds pain.

I want to dance despite thunder thighs and piano legs. There's rhythm buried in these hips. I've been teased, like you. I've watched the thin bodies dance in pink leotards in the infinite mirror of childhood. I've stood there and felt strong until I stumbled. Until I felt my body unable to mimic the other bodies in the room. Where does shame come from and where does it live? Is it a river we carry, a place we must come to bathe inside ourselves?

Give me

the blunt brink   climbers prefer
an edge   to grip
violent tip   into palm
pain as I rise   breath sharp

I believe body is the only truth. A truth that softens like stone between my fucking fingers—not my fucking fingers, the fingers I use to fuck. The light like this off the raw and untumbled, the semi-precious: here, then gone, then here again. This, like making love: another woman here, then gone, then here again.

As if we have anyone between our fingers for very long.

Perhaps all I need is to allow, to turn toward a well-planned meal in response to something not quite hunger more like *fill me*, realize my body is begging to be fed to be whole to be holy. To become the space between who I thought I was in blue absence, and this becoming like a predator circling the edges of the suburbs as they encroach on the last wild space. My body, a soft opening, a rolling meadow, a sad and joyful ecstasy, a big giant mistake, and, like the hills of Tara in Ireland: a fortress. Like the Hindu goddess: a ferry. A woman of many arms and hands that reach and say *here, come with me, we are all good. So, so good.*

She is coming back to food after loss. She is afraid of how to sit and eat. Feel satiated. Enjoy and offer, cook and lean back in the chair, hand in her lover's lap, smile, sip water and wine, say *thank you.*

Thank you, wrinkled skin where fat used to be, and will return. Thank you years of grief-stricken thinness, thank you blue days when I consider addiction to stay this way. Thank you disorder. Thank you craving.

Oh, dis-order. Oh well-planned mess I call art. Consider this: when I was in grief I wanted nothing, no food in my mouth. Only air. Only blue blue sky, an empty gut and more air, more blue and a blue blue mouth, the holier mouth, the darker blue the blue between the thighs, you. Oh holy hunger, thank you. I court you when I want something from another, when my body is a feminine thing, all waste and water and struggle for attention.

Watch as I walk the lonely streets now still crying. I feel full. I want to be light. Light me up. Let me turn your body over in this bed and forget hunger, use this scarf to tie our drunken hands to the bed posts and make light of you. I remember light. I remember grief like an earthquake living a long life in my connective tissues. Oh, fascia, oh holy shaking, oh yearning, oh open-armed body a beg to be made light. *Make me light.* Oh body oh empty container make me light oh dark apartment oh new lover and other lover and then no, not that lover but this lover make me light.

I prefer my life to cradle nothing, but how silly.

Let me be this, too: the OH how goddamn good it felt for a while to want what was wrong for me, how I chose the quake more than once, just to see how long I could hold onto the doorframe and endure.

                              Give me
                the turquoise   hidden
                agate   before polish
              geode   before body slam
          something rough   imperfect

For a while, just me and the dog and the night and some blue mountain view, how I thought it would last, the emptiness like a good drug—the kind we took in the woods to meet the god of our early erotic understanding, so young then our hunger for expansion and sex like a false spring, both the season and the water coming down the red and salty canyon. Now, my sadness is over. Or, she's full. Or, I just want her back. Make me both. Light and blue, steady and shaking just long enough to make something I'm proud of. I don't want to starve, or turn away from good, or cut my skin like I did at twenty-three. I never wasted away, really, but oh how I miss the excitement of working so hard at a thing I knew I'd never have. Of being wasted. Sometimes, I miss my grief like the holy man misses god in the long dark night after ecstasy, that place where we realize we have to wake up, make the coffee, do the laundry, be of this world despite knowing in our bones the truth we reach when we barely survive—I have barely survived this. I have circled the block again and again and again. Let me forget hunger, just a little longer. Let me keep walking.

                              Let me
                endure slice   not slip
            embrace blood's   slow trickle
                  embody   resistance
              climb anyway   unprepared

Now, days are anything but typical—days are a question I love, a sermon I must attend or I'll forget how to put my hands together and sing. Or scream. Both prayers. The sliding glass door is open and my body faces a day that is raining and sunny, both. It's cold *and* warm. I feel ease for once. Joy in the raindrops as they sparkle in the sun on their way down. Notice my body is a sky. The Colorado seasons opening at once: the word *simultaneous*, a cliché—metaphors I overuse that perhaps aren't metaphors, just stories I keep telling, everything that blusters through this brain an offering. I want my life to be an offering. Goddamn it. Can't you see me standing here in this little yard, cement and grass, by this little mountain, the base of bigger mountains the Rocky mountains the mountain of my heart screaming *I am sky.* I am something those chatty magpies fly through every multi-seasonal day—I move forward just an inch because I have to, even though chaos is gone, the day just a day. I push against everything and everything pushes back.

Dear Me As I Try To Remember Something About Love

Remember when you said to love is still the most radical act.
Remember when you were heartbroken by love and laughed at that bullshit
 line.
Remember when you said you'd never get on Tinder, cut your hair, paint
 anything gray again.
Remember when you said you'd never stay with a lover who didn't make love,
 then you did.
Remember in Middle School when you watched the Titanic and the Leo
 version of Romeo and Juliet.
Remember how you played the soundtracks over and over and looked out the
 window.
Remember when you wrote a poem about a kid you wished would love you like
 that.
Remember how you used this form, then: *remember the way you talked to me,*
 remember the way you set me free, remember how we skated to the song,
 remember how you wished it was too long...
Remember how Mr. Doerwaldt read it aloud in class and it was that day in
 8th grade you became a poet and also the one who drooled her feelings all
 over the halls, an animal unable to hide.
Remember when mom made fun of you for loving Titanic and Romeo and
 Juliet and how you fell in love with Leo AND Kate AND Claire.
Remember Celine Dion, too, how you loved her husband ballads.
Remember how much you love love all over the place. The power of love. You
 jump I jump jack. Married at, like, twelve and the perfect loss of virginity
 under white sheets and enchanted parties with coy eyes turning corners
 and don't forget how much you still stand in elevators waiting to be pinned.
Remember dead on top of one another, love for the sake of love despite
 family and empire, poison in the mouth and poison in the body and love you
 would die for and the professor who called out the historical context and
 gender problems in this, how hormones were at play and you know you
 would have married anyone at, like, twelve if they would have loved you like
 that.
Remember my heart will go on and the room on that damn door and the
 way the orchestra played as the ship sank and how much you wanted to
 make love in a car on a sinking ship.
Remember how you've always known love and tragedy are the same.
Remember how this became a hunger you still can't name, how you starved

yourself and purged and snorted stolen pain pills and laid at night with your
diary and your pen writing *love me* in a thousand different ways.

Remember this now, as you find yourself revived after loss. A revelation. A
tragedy and a blonde body in your bed, the bed your ex bought you so you
could go far away from the home she kept.

Remember that you still think love is radical despite how you were asked to
leave a home that was yours, with nothing, and did—as in, how do we
keep doing this, as in, how after divorce and children and contracts and
shared utensils do people find themselves saying yes again and again.

Remember the first time you realized how fucked we all are (thank you therapy)
because our bodies can only relate the way we were taught to relate.

Remember when you realized how much work you have to do here.

Remember climbing into a car with your dog and a friend driving a van with
only the things you could fit, your books and stones and some clothes, a
chair, a few plants, a bottle of 10-year anniversary wine you did not make it
to from Mount Vesuvius, your old cat that will not die, the land with the
dogs and goats left behind staring back as you drove to the next season of
your life.

Remember the rebound lover, so much like your father. Or someone.

Remember how your body, finally, wasted away.

Remember how much you wanted the tragedy, if you're honest.

Remember how you're often not very honest.

Remember the concave of your belly, how you stared and fell in love with your
body like that.

Remember drinking that whole bottle of Italian wine, drunk with the friend
who got you here.

Remember sitting on her porch taking photos and making Tinder profiles.

Remember the mistake of the wrong spell.

Remember heartbreak that felt like the other heartbreak and the pain a rubber
band ball and how much you forgot the love like Leo and Claire and instead
for a while loved like two people dancing on a gay bar's dance floor after the
lights come on, kissing but missing and falling all the way home.

Remember how much you believe in words.

Remember radical.

Remember the blonde girl with great dewy skin (that's a thing now) on the bar
stool across from you, both your hands around glasses of whiskey, her jean
jacket and feminist enamel pins and her open mouth laughing her open

hands her open.

Remember when you said you'd never love someone younger than you,
definitely not this young, and definitely not so blonde and so happy.

Remember when you thought you'd be the one who knew the most about
music and books.

Remember the body is radical is a thing that breathes that pumps, is resuscitation.

Remember how far away you put your pleasure, how easy your tongue found
her way back to skin.

Remember how often you say never again, or this now, or here.

Remember how the best love shows up and smiles every time, is herself: a
body nervous and a voice like a cheerleader like you when you're happy
do you remember happy and a hope like a floating ship like desire that
floods everything that is a preteen lying in her bed with soundtracks from
love stories remember what it feels like to see a woman who will not sink.

Remember her laugh like a galaxy.

Remember her pink lips, how you kissed by the car, how she'll always claim she
kissed you first.

Remember how fun it is to say no, it was me, and this be foreplay.

Remember how free you wanted to feel, how the blonde dewy galaxy gives you
this, then takes you home and makes food, plays records, dances around the
room with your dog and says *what can I do better* when you find yourself
on the floor lost in time, sobs like the Shenandoah like the red mud in New
Mexico after a flash flood your old land wet, spilling out of every pore

Remember when you kissed her and felt every cell naked in a snowstorm.

Remember this when you want to say go, leave me be, I can't.

Remember the year you spent in your bathtub, the two months of hives, the
clothes a dance around your skin, the fires you lit in that tiny apartment
the attempt at polyamory the warehouse parties and couples surrounding
you at dawn to see if you'd come home and make their bed more fun, the
DMT, the open mics you never really liked the tight fist you didn't know
you held now loose and slapping ass all over a new city remember what it
felt like to sink and be light and want to ignite fire from the very thighs of
you.

Remember the yellow tulips she brought the first time she came to you.

Remember how the grip leaves. How it returns.

Remember her pink lips, the yellow tulips, the miracle of her body on your bed.

Remember when you said love must be work. Then when you said it must be easy.

Remember when you fell in love with a woman 8 years your younger, how you dressed up like Leo and Claire, how you became the party, the whole Capulet mansion, how the black light lit you up as the Halloween costumes faded to black around you, how you felt like this can't be love at 35, and it is.

Remember how much you believe in this, even though it hurts, even though nothing is certain.

Remember most of all remember your body and all the crush in her, the way she laid awake at night under her pink quilt on the mountain road, her littleness lost forever: a love song a ballad that will not end

Goat Memory

I grab your hoof in my hand at dawn,
wrap a leather cord around the wiry fur
at your ankle and attach it to the stand
so you don't kick me. Then, hungry goat,
as you dip your face into the feed bucket,
I slide the head latch over the space
around your neck to keep you here.
Your warm purple teat in my hand,
the sound of dawn a slow lesson
I am learning and relearning,
your rushed and happy chomping
of alfalfa pellets near my ear—
this is a love I didn't know I needed.
And the milk as I work, it's warm
like warm and sweet like sweet,
clean like clean. This must be
what Buddhists mean by *isness*
because as I form my hand
into a kind of mouth, cup
my fingers high at the base
of your udder and poke around
like a kid would to coax the milk
to let go, I am in awe, every time,
when you do. I am only this human
who wants something from you,
and you are an animal—tamed,
valuable. Beautiful. You fill my jar
and I scratch your chin, let you go.
There is more to this, I know,
a relationship I am careful
not to exploit. You are well fed,
and so am I. Each morning
I am tired and ready to give you
a break, dry you up. And then

we sit together again. You eat
and I lean my head against
your many bellies. Inside,
your rumen ferments so loudly
I invent little cocktail parties
for all the microbes and bacteria
within you—live fermentation
like a festival in the dark—
together we digest these lives
we were given. For now,
I want to give in
to this illusion
of safety. All is
as it is as it is.

Tara Shea Burke is a queer poet and teacher from the Blue Ridge Mountains and Hampton Roads, Virginia. She's a writing instructor, editor, creative coach, and yoga teacher who has taught and lived in Virginia, New Mexico, and Colorado. Her writing has appeared in *Erase the Patriarchy*, a book of sexual assault and rape erasures, edited by Isobel O'Hare and University of Hell Press, and *Reading Queer, Poetry in the Time of Chaos*, edited by Neil de la Flor and Maureen Seaton from Anhinga Press, as well as many journals and anthologies. She is a board member for Sinister Wisdom, the longest running multicultural, lesbian literary and arts journal, where she learns how to have powerful, evolving, inclusive conversations about body, sexuality, identity, and accessible art. She believes in community building and radical support for any human that wants to tell their stories, and has edited and coached writers through creative work, dissertations, personal projects, and movement-based writing for healing and growth. In the academic classroom, she wants her first year college students to feel supported more that they feel critiqued, and learn how to use their voices to become active, engaged, and if lucky, radical citizens of this earth. To find more about her writing and work visit www.tarasheaburke.com

www.ingramcontent.com/pod-product-compliance
Lightning Source LLC
Chambersburg PA
CBHW021157090426

42740CB00008B/1129